THE
COUNTRY
DIARY®

Stencilling

in the style of

The Edwardian Lady

Projects designed and created by Ashe Ericksson
Original illustrations by Edith Holden

The Country Diary of an Edwardian Lady®
© Rowena Stott (Designs) Ltd and RW.UK Ltd 2006
Licensed by ©opyrights Group
Original Illustrations by Edith Holden

KUDOS

First published in Great Britain in 2006 by Kudos, an imprint of Top That! Publishing plc,
Marine House, Tide Mill Way, Woodbridge, Suffolk IP12 1AP, UK
www.kudosbooks.com

0 2 4 6 8 9 7 5 3 1

ISBN 1-84666-018-1

A catalogue record for this book is available from the British Library
Colour reproduction by Reflex Reproduction
Printed and bound in China

Acknowledgments and Credits:
Managing Director Barrie Henderson
Kudos Manager Mike Saiz
Designer James Rous
Senior Editor Karen Rigden
Junior Editor Duncan Ballantyne-Way
Photographer Jo Broome
Projects designed and created by Ashe Ericksson
Picture Credits: Page 13, Abode Interiors Picture Library

Contents

Introduction

Only stencilling has the ability to transform a dull piece of furniture or dreary area of wall and make it look fresh and rejuvenated. Appealing to the beginner as well as the experienced practitioner, this craft will bring delight to the bare spaces you choose to stencil.

Stencilling has grown in popularity in recent years, due largely to the impact of make-over shows which use stencilling as a quick and cheap way of transforming an old or drab piece of furniture. But there is still much to be explored, and it is worth searching through your garage or attic and looking to see if a chair or table you'd previously stashed away could turn out to be the perfect subject for stencilling.

You'll be surprised at the many places where stencilling can be performed, and the objects which can be transformed by the subtle layering of paint. From flower pots and vases to blankets and children's chairs there is nothing like personalising old belongings and presents for those you hold dear.

However, it is important to know the procedures involved and the materials that are required to ensure your attempts are successful, and

that you don't end up ruining a perfectly good item. This book will help ensure you get the best results as each project has been researched and performed by a professional and, if the step-by-steps are followed carefully, you're sure to create stunning items for your home.

Inspired by the beautiful paintings of Edith Holden, the stencil designs featured in this book are based directly on the watercolours of *The Country Diary*.

It comes as no surprise that the artwork of *The Country Diary* has transferred into stencilling designs so successfully. The simplicity and clarity of the paintings make them an ideal stencilling source, and if there is an image in the diary which you think will work particularly well with a blanket or chair then try making your own stencil. It is always worth experimenting to find out what looks best.

Edith Holden –
A Brief Biography

Edith Holden was born in 1871, and lived most of her life as an artist and art teacher. She was also renowned for her illustrations to popular children's books. Although *The Country Diary of an Edwardian Lady*® was published in 1977, it is actually a naturalist's diary for the year 1906. In the course of that year, Edith Holden recorded the changes to British flora and fauna through the seasons, in words and delicate, delightful watercolours.

Since the seventies, readers have been captivated by the diary's charm and its evocation of a simpler world. It has now been translated into 13 different languages and sold millions of copies worldwide. Tragically, Edith died in 1920, at the age of 49. Collecting flowers from a riverbank in Richmond near London, she fell into the River Thames and drowned.

Materials and Equipment

The versatility of stencilling and the wide range of materials that can be used ensures that as an art form, it is impossible not to express your own individuality whilst stencilling.

There are innumerable choices to make when choosing your materials for stencilling.

Essentially the key things to consider are what type of surface you will be stencilling and what purpose it will serve in the future. For instance, a cushion will need completely different paints to a wall. Having said that, acrylic paint is incredibly versatile and can be used on almost any surface, so it is a great medium to begin with. The next few pages offer a comprehensive guide to the materials used in the featured projects – and more, so you can continue to experiment beyond this book.

Stencil Material

Perhaps the most consistently useful stencil materials are clear acetate sheets. These allow you to see what you are doing as well as being ideal material for repeated patterns or multiple stencil designs which need to be lined up. However acetate is prone to splitting on occasions so be careful when deciding on the thickness you want. Generally, it is advisable for you to choose a medium thickness which will possess both malleability and strength.

Coloured, plastic stencil card is another choice. Generally much thicker than acetate, it is therefore less prone to tearing but it is harder to cut so is best used for simple designs. Being coloured it can also be harder to position correctly.

Oiled manilla card is the traditional material used in stencilling. It is better suited to large projects as it won't flop about as much as acetate. Unlike either of the plastic materials it is completely opaque so positioning can be tricky.

Brushes and Sponges

You can apply your paint however you want – even with your fingers – however, most of the the time you'll use either a brush or sponge. Stencil brushes have a short clump of bristles cut flat at the end. The stippling action with these brushes means that there is less risk of paint seeping under the stencil. It is worth seeking out good-quality stencil brushes that feel soft but firm and not too stiff. Many jobs will need two to four brushes in various sizes; use separate brushes for different colours and give each a good rinse in clean water between colour applications.

As well as stipple brushes of different sizes it is a good idea to have one fine artist's brush for touching up and detailing. You should also have a large decorator's brush for backgrounds and one medium-sized varnishing brush.

The same advice applies to sponges, as it is useful to have a few different sizes and also textures to create different effects.

Paints

The right choice of paint can be the difference between a successful stencil and a poor one. However, try experimenting on different surfaces with a variety of paints; you might just find an effect no one else has discovered!

There are so many paints that can be used for stencilling that it can be hard to know where to start. All the paints can be broadly divided into two groups: water-based or oil-based.

Water-based paints are useful when stencilling large areas because they dry quickly. That also means that any mistake you make is irreparable unless you correct it quickly.

Oil-based paints come in either sticks, crayons or pots. Oil-based paints take a long time to dry so it is easy to rectify any mistakes. They are also perfect for blending colours. However, if you are using multiple stencils for one design it can make the process very slow as you wait for colours to dry.

Oil-based paints are easy to control and won't bleed underneath the stencil making a mess of your lines. The disadvantage is that they smudge easily, and if possible they should never be used on wood.

This book hasn't used all of the paints on the market but aims instead to give a good grounding in how to use the most common and versatile water-soluble paints, such as acrylic, fabric and spray paints (plus a few others).

Acrylic Paints

Popular, versatile and accessible, acrylic paints come in a multitude of colours and dry reasonably quickly. Acrylic paints are perfect for beginners as they can be used on almost any surface, from metal and fabric, to wood and plaster.

Water-soluble while wet, acrylic paints can be easily mixed and they dry to a smooth, plastic-like finish depending on your work surface. Use them straight from the tube with a damp rather than a wet brush, keep kitchen roll to hand to remove excess water after rinsing.

Fabric Paints

While acrylic paint can be used on fabric, specifically designed paint is easier to use and has a better finish. Each brand does vary, though, and to make the item washable fabric paints normally require a mordant, sealant or heat to fix. So read the manufacturer's instructions first.

Spray Paints

Spray paints should be handled with care because they are toxic. They create a pleasant hazy effect and are excellent for experimenting and can be used on various surfaces depending on the make. Most are water-based but there are a number of varieties including metallic,

pearlised, enamel or frosted finishes for glass and mirror (see page 24). If you like working with spray paints it is also worth trying the two-step effect paints that are available as well.

More Mediums

If you wish to use oil-based paints and other mediums read on in this section to get the basics then just follow the advice on the packaging and experiment.

Gouache Paints

Giving more vibrant and denser colours than acrylic, gouache paint does, however, need to be sealed with varnish.

Stencil Crayons

These are oil-based paints in stick form, created specifically for stencilling. They are expensive but they last for ages and do not dry out.

Ceramic and Porcelain Paints

Ceramic and porcelain paints are tricky to master as they have a thin consistency, so practise on old kitchen tiles first. It is important to read the manufacturer's instructions before purchase as some require special varnishes or techniques to fix them, such as placing your item in the oven.

Techniques

You will find that the more stencilling you do the more techniques and nuances you'll pick up by yourself. Here are a few basic techniques to cement the knowledge of the skilled practitioner as well benefiting the novice just starting out.

Using Templates

The beauty of stencils is that you don't have to be a gifted artist to get great results, every time. While some people may feel confident enough to design and draw their own motifs it is far easier to buy ready-made stencils or, as this book demonstrates, cut your own using pre-drawn templates.

Each of the projects later in this book have specially designed templates that can be photocopied (or scanned – if you have a scanner – and adjusted on your computer) to an appropriate size and used as an outline for your own stencils. Once photocopied, you can use a permanent marker pen to draw around the outline of the template onto your stencil material.

If you don't have access to either a photocopier or scanner, trace your source material then draw a grid over the top of the design. On a separate piece of paper, draw a larger or smaller grid roughly the size you want the design to be then in each square carefully draw the outline of the stencil as it appears in that box.

Cutting the Stencil

A sharp craft knife or scalpel are the best tools to use for cutting stencil material. Anything else generally isn't sharp enough and could result in injury.

Never cut a stencil without having a cutting mat, board or piece of thick cardboard underneath and ensure your surface is completely flat – a purpose-made cutting mat is the best material to cut on as it has more give and won't blunt the blade.

Always cut towards your body so you can control the knife but keep your other hand out of the way in case the blade should slip. Try to keep your line clean and crisp; a badly cut stencil will give your work a rough outline.

Securing the Stencil

For the best results possible you need to keep your stencil in place as you apply the paint. Masking tape, (not sticky tape) can be used to stick down the edges of the stencil.

However, a far better way to keep your stencil in place is to use low-tack glue in an aerosol can – there are several to choose from on the market. These sprays will ensure that nearly all of the stencil comes into contact with your work surface which will help prevent the paint seeping underneath the acetate and spoiling your design. The other benefit to spray glue is that is can be removed relatively easily, minimising the damage to the work surface. Be warned! The peeled off stencil will remain tacky afterwards and has a habit of sticking to other papers and stencils.

Registration Marks

Simple stencil designs will use one sheet of acetate and only a few colours. However, more complex designs use several sheets of acetate, which, when layered on top of each other, build up to create one picture. This allows you to use several colours and develop more intricate details in the motif. The stencilling process is essentially no different but to ensure that your layers line up with each other registration marks can be used. These are simply points that are drawn onto uncut areas of the acetate that indicate the key points in the design in previous layers, for instance the corners of a border. See page 37 for more information and for registration marks in use.

Paint Application

A brush or a sponge can be used to apply your paint, depending on the effect you want to achieve or the area of work you are stencilling. Whatever your choice they must be dry and clean. Overloading your brush will smudge your design. Regularly clean your brush or sponge to stop it clogging up. Always try to apply the paint around the edge of the cut out area first.

The paint can be applied in two ways, stippling or swirling. To stipple, hold the brush at a right angle to the stencil and gently dab the paint onto the design. Alternatively, to use the swirl technique, use a circular swirling motion when applying the paint to the stencil openings.

Taking Care of your Stencils

If you want to use your stencils again, it pays to take a bit of care over them. When using acrylic paint try to wash it off with water as soon as you're done – if you leave it too long it will be permanent. It can be scratched off, but this is likely to tear the acetate. For other paints try methylated spirits on a bit of cotton wool if water doesn't work.

When storing your stencils, use a low-tack tape or glue (they may even be sticky enough from the aerosol glue) to stick them onto sheets of paper or thin card and keep flat. This will prevent them sticking together or getting bent.

Before use, but after cutting, you can strengthen delicate stencils by applying a coat of acrylic varnish on both sides of the stencil.

Repairing Stencils

During cutting or while using your stencils you're bound to get a few tears. Depending on the severity of the tear (sometimes you'll just have to cut a new stencil) you can patch the rip with sticky tape. Make sure you trim back any excess or it will effect your design.

Troubleshooting

Although using a stencil does enable you to repeat a uniform design or create an image you couldn't otherwise generate by hand, problems do occur. Most common is paint bleeding under the stencil and ruining the clean line of the design. While wet, a clean brush or cotton bud dipped in water or methylated spirits can be used to tidy up the line.

Once dry, however, it really depends on the surface you're working on: if you have a coloured base coat use this paint to cover up your mistake, or, if you are working directly onto the surface you may be able to scrape off the unwanted paint with a craft knife.

These tricks can be used on most hard, non-porous surfaces. Mistakes on fabric, though, can rarely be salvaged. In these instances try adapting the design by painting freehand.

To avoid these problems in the first place make sure you aren't working with an overly wet brush or runny paint. Keep kitchen paper to hand to remove any excess water especially after rinsing your brush or sponge. On repeat pattern designs, regularly check the back of your stencil for blobs of paint, cleaning the acetate as needed.

Paint Effects – Creating Depth and Contrast

Some simple shading can add depth and contrast to your designs with minimal difficulty. All you have to do is put more paint on the outside of the pattern than on the inside. A clever use of the swirling technique produces similar effects.

A Faded Effect

A faded effect can add great charm to your design and make it seem as though it has been part of the furniture for years. Using a sponge, dab it into the paint so that it doesn't pick up too much colour. Do a thorough practice before launching into your stencil.

Alternatively, you can create a different faded effect by cautiously removing some of the paint with sandpaper to give a worn surface.

Colour Blending

This effect doesn't refer to mixing paints but rather the technique to achieve subtle changes of colour. Blending couldn't be easier, it merely involves using a dirty brush to get unsystematic alterations in colour.

Colour Mixing

With the primary colours of blue, yellow and red and the addition of white you can mix almost any colour you want. The best way to learn how to create different shades is to experiment. As a basic guide use the chart below which begins to show the different colours you can create using the acrylic paints supplied in this kit. Vary the quantities and you'll have an even broader spectrum, so give it a go!

Once you've explored the potential of mixing two colours, experiment further and introduce a third or even add another mixed colour.	Cadmium Yellow	Alizarin Crimson	Raw Umber	Ultramarine	White
Cadmium Yellow					
Alizarin Crimson					
Raw Umber					
Ultramarine					
White					

Preparations and Finishes

Getting the very best project you can isn't just about careful stencilling; selecting the right base coat or varnish is important too. Here's a guide to help you decide what to use and when.

Emulsion Paints

Emulsion paint is available in both matt and silk finishes, and is generally used as a good base coat for working on wood or plaster. You can stencil with it but its thin consistency makes it prone to drips.

Liming Wax

Also known as whitewash pickling stain, liming wax is a smooth paste wax formulation that produces a pale finish and allows the wood grain to show through. Particularly effective on oak and other open grain woods, it is available in several colours.

Liming wax can be applied directly onto bare wood using a paintbrush. It can be used on some stained and sealed surfaces. Some woods will benefit from opening the grain with a wire brush.

Acrylic Paint

The use of acrylic paint extends to base coats as well. Use it on surfaces as you would with stencilling (see page 8).

Varnishes

Varnish is a necessary step in making your work lasting and durable. The choice of varnish is dependant upon the surface you're stencilling on and the look you want to achieve.

Looking on the shelves it can be a complete mystery as to which varnish to pick. Essentially there are four types of varnish: alkyd, polyurethane, spar and quick-drying.

Alkyds are the traditional varnishes made from a polyester resin. These varnishes are durable, flexible, resistant to abrasion, have good adhesion qualities, are resistant to discolouration from UV and light, and are relatively less expensive than the other varnishes. Their only negative is that they are very slow drying and will take 24 hours to dry sufficiently for recoating. For this reason alone, the alkyd varnishes are becoming difficult to find as a furniture finish, but their superior qualities make them the choice for floor finishing varnishes.

Polyurethane resins have replaced the alkyds for only one reason – they dry faster. They are also more water resistant. However, several of the benefits of the alkyds have been sacrificed. Polyurethane varnishes are not light and UV resistant, and therefore can turn yellow.

Spar varnish is a formulation of phenolic and alkyd resins in tung oil. Spar varnish is a relatively hard finish with superior water resistance and flexibility. It has a good resistance to damage from either acid or alkaline substances or deterioration from light and UV. Unfortunately, it is very slow drying and it has a naturally deep yellow colour.

Fast-drying, or VT (vinyl toluene), varnishes have been modified with styrene resins to produce a very fast drying time that is similar to that of a nitrocellulose lacquer. This speed comes with the sacrifice of the protective properties found in the other varnishes. Of these four varieties polyurethane varnishes are most common for indoor use.

Choose from matt, satin or gloss finishes with any of these varieties, where possible selecting the varnish to suit the material you're stencilling on. Specialised decorator's varnishes will give you the best results and are often multi-purpose.

Advance Finishes

The aesthetic reason for most effects is to give your finished piece an aged appearance. There are a number of techniques that don't feature in this book which you may wish to try for yourself.

Waxing

Adding a coat of tinted wax after stencilling can be the easiest way to add a mellow finish to your projects. Use a natural-coloured wax or a staining wax over the top of the last coat of varnish (you'll get the best look if the last coat of varnish has a matt finish). Coloured waxes will naturally alter the colour of your work so bear this in mind. Follow the manufacturer's instructions wherever possible or simply rub on the wax with a soft cloth and leave for thirty minutes before buffing with a clean cloth.

Antiquing

Antiquing is a simple paint effect, created by using raw umber acrylic paint diluted in plenty of water. The antique wash should be added after two coats of varnish have completely dried – for the brush work to stand out it needs a varnish base but you still need further coats of varnish to give depth to the overall finish.

Using a stiff-bristled brush, and being careful not to overload it with the umber wash, brush it over the project. Delaying briefly, but not so long the wash dries, use a cloth to wipe off some of the colour leaving more in certain places. A softer look can be achieved by applying the wash with a soft cloth.

Crackle Glazes

Crackle varnishes are generally a two-step process whereby the first layer of varnish is slow-drying (normally oil-based). Onto this a second varnish is applied which is quick drying (normally water-soluble). The difference in the drying times causes the upper varnish to crack.

In the shops you'll find aerosol cans of crackle glaze. These aren't particularly suited to stencilling as the two stages use coloured varnishes, and the application of the second will obscure much of your work. For the best results choose the crackle glazes specifically designed for decoupage and stencilling. These two varnishes dry clear and the definition of the cracks is shown up by rubbing raw umber oil paint into the cracks. Coats of clear varnish can then be applied on top of either product to finish your piece.

— Stencilling on Walls —

This book demonstrates the versatility of stencils with projects that feature metal, wood, glass, fabric and of course, plaster. However, people's first thoughts of stencilling are of designs on walls and a detailed project is featured on page 54. With this project and any others you choose to create yourself, you'll need to do a bit of preparation and planning beforehand. Below is a brief guide to stencilling on walls that should help you get great results.

Although walls do not need to be perfectly smooth, all traces of wallpaper should be removed and significant indentations filled in.

If you want to stencil onto bare plaster, you should treat it with a universal sealant first.

Allow all treatments or paints to dry completely before starting your work or your results could look patchy or even flake off.

Measuring your Wall

When you have decided the approximate height at which you want your design, you will need to establish the true height of the wall (see diagram far right).

A plumb line uses gravity to find a perfectly straight line from the ceiling. It is simple to use and will help you get the first stencil perfectly straight, which then ensures the rest of the design is in line too. You can buy plumb lines from all hardware or DIY stores but it is easy to make your own, just cut a piece of string shorter than your wall and tie a dense object to one end, such as a large screw or ring.

Find the centre point of the wall by crossing over two pieces of string from opposing corners – pin them to the wall corners. Where the strings cross is the centre point. When this is done hold the string end of the plumb line at the point where the wall meets the ceiling and let the weight hang down. Once you line up the plumb line with the centre point, you have an exact line from the middle of the wall to the ceiling.

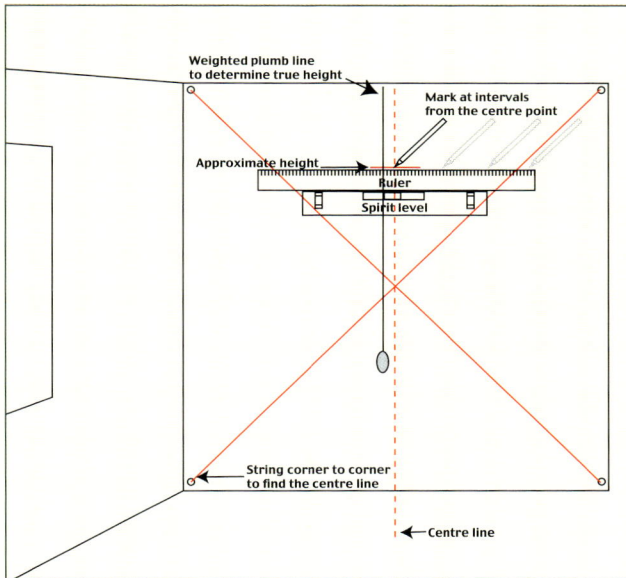

Weighted plumb line to determine true height

Mark at intervals from the centre point

Approximate height

Ruler

Spirit level

String corner to corner to find the centre line

Centre line

Hot Tips

• *Old houses with uneven ceilings and floors are better suited to an irregular stencil pattern, that does not work along strict vertical and horizontal lines.*

• *Remember to use a plumb line and spirit level when working around fixtures such as windows, sockets and radiators.*

It is then just a question of measuring from the plumb line, using a spirit level to get vertical and horizontal markers, and marking them with a pencil. If you then place a ruler – making sure that it's straight by resting it on top of a spirit level – and place it horizontally across your measurements, you can mark at equal intervals from the centre line outwards in the space on either side of the plumb line.

Corners

It is unlikely that a repeated design will fit perfectly to the length of your wall. You can hide this by subtly varying the length of the gaps between each repetition. If this is done well, the eye will not notice.

Alternatively, you can use a different design at either end of the wall to act as 'bookends' for the main feature. Another option, and one that has a certain organic appeal, is to take elements from the original design and combine them into a corner motif.

Flower Pot

Stencilling is a great way to decorate your home inside and out. While the basic technique remains the same, it's best to start with small, manageable projects, like this flower pot, until you have perfected the skill – you'll also be able to see and appreciate your efforts right away.

Materials and Equipment
Paper, Masking tape, Acetate, Marker pen
Craft knife, Cutting mat, Terra cotta pot,
Spray glue, Old tile or container, Water and container,
Stencil brush, Matt varnish

Paint: Acrylic
White, Red, Yellow and Blue. Optional: Yellow ochre and Green

1. Trace or photocopy the template on page 22, altering the size to fit onto your flower pot. Tape this copy beneath a sheet of acetate and draw the outline of the design.

2. On a cutting mat, cut around the outline with your craft knife. If using a large piece of acetate, measure the rim of your pot and trim the stencil to a more manageable size.

3. Secure your stencil to the rim of the pot. You could use masking tape but this example uses a spray glue so the acetate is completely in contact with the surface.

4. Using an old tile as a palette, begin mixing white and red acrylic paint to make a pale pink. Don't mix the paint completely, variations in tone will look effective.

5. Using a stencil brush, apply the pink paint in a dabbing motion. Don't overload the brush with paint or it could then seep under the acetate.

6. Mix up two shades of green from the blue and yellow paint, apply these to the leaves, keeping the two tones distinct. Use a smaller brush if you find it easier to handle.

7. Using a small paint brush, add the yellow pollen to the flowers. If you struggled to cut the holes from the acetate these can be touched up or painted freehand afterwards.

8. Leave the paint to dry slightly to prevent smudging as you remove the stencil. Spray again with the glue then reposition to continue the design around the rim.

9. Continue to paint the design as before with the pink, greens and yellow centres. Use a combination of stencil brushes and artist brushes.

10. To protect your design, especially if it's going outside, apply at least two coats of matt varnish, or as recommended by the manufacturer. A wood varnish will suffice if you can't find one for terra cotta.

Stencil Template and Colour Guide

Glass Vase

While acrylics can be considered the 'wonder paint' of the stencilling world there are still plenty of fabulous paints that should be experimented with. This project uses a frosting spray that's easy to use and gives stunning results that couldn't be achieved with acrylic paint. A similar effect could be created on a mirror, or why not try other glass surfaces such as a window?

Materials and Equipment

Paper, Sticky/masking tapes, Acetate, Marker pen,
Craft knife, Cutting mat, Glass vase,
Methylated spirits, Spray glue, Newspaper,

Paint: Spray Paint

Glass frosting spray paint

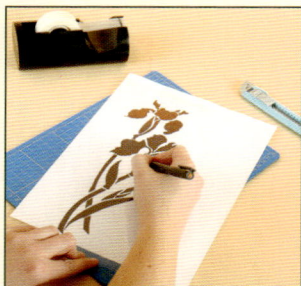

1. Trace or photocopy the iris design on page 26, enlarging as necessary. Tape the copy onto the reverse of a sheet of acetate and draw the outline with the marker pen.

2. Using a craft knife, carefully cut out the iris outline on a cutting mat. Remember to cut towards your body so you keep control of the blade.

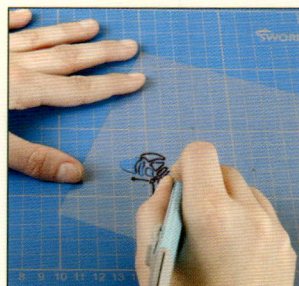

3. Repeat steps one and two to cut out the small butterfly stencil that will feature on the sides of the vase. Trim both stencils to comfortably fit onto the vase.

4. Clean the vase with methylated spirits and an old rag or paper towel so that the surface is free from dirt and grease.

5. Spray the iris stencil with adhesive and smooth down to ensure there are no gaps for the frosting spray to seep into (although if drifting occurs see step 9).

6. With any spray paint it's important to mask off areas you don't want to paint. Use newspaper and masking tape to completely cover the rest of the vase.

7. Spray the frosting paint evenly in a well-ventilated area in accordance with the manufacturer's instructions. Unless directed otherwise one coat should be enough.

8. Once dry remove the masking paper and stencil. Repeat the process with the butterfly stencil placing one on two of the sides; one at the top, one on the bottom.

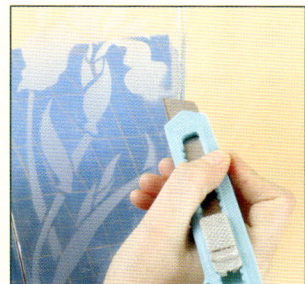

9. If the frosting spray has drifted, the design can be tidied up using a cotton bud and methylated spirits or by scraping off the paint carefully with a craft knife.

Stencil Templates

Autumn Throw

Fabric and stencils may not seem like an obvious combination but by using fabric paints you can create beautiful effects simply. Fabric paints are easy to get hold of but make sure you read the instructions before use and check the type of material you're using to ensure they're compatible.

Materials and Equipment

Paper, Sticky tape, Acetate, Marker pen Craft knife, Cutting mat,
Old tile or container, Water and container,
Plain throw or blanket (washed and dried), Spray glue, Stencil brush,
Mordant (read manufacturer's instructions for how to fix the fabric paints)

Paint: Fabric
Blue, Red, Yellow, Green and White

1. Trace or photocopy the template on page 30, enlarging if necessary. Place under a sheet of acetate and draw over the outline of the stencil.

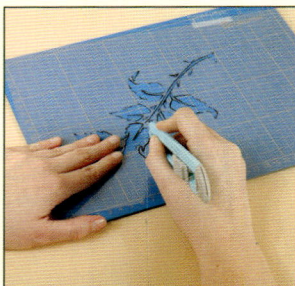

2. Carefully cut out the design on a cutting mat using a craft knife. Make sure the serrated edges of the leaves are sharp in appearance.

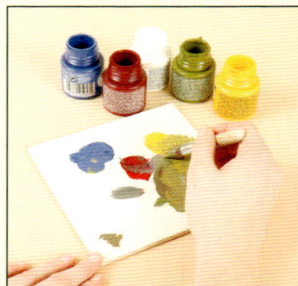

3. Select and mix your fabric paints to create subtle browns and greens. Just like acrylic paints you can achieve several shades by mixing the primary or basic colours.

4. Spray the stencil with glue and smooth down onto the throw. This is the trickiest part as the stencil won't lie as flat on fabric, use masking tape as well if need be.

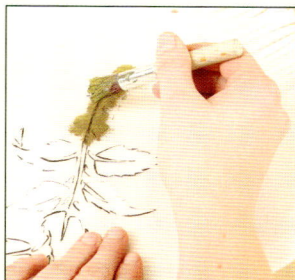

5. Begin painting with your premixed paint. Depending on the weave and texture of the throw you will have to apply the paint thinly or thickly.

6. Continue to add more colour but don't clean your brush in between applications; just allow the colours to blend and change subtly.

7. Complete the leaf design, and leave to dry slightly before peeling off carefully.

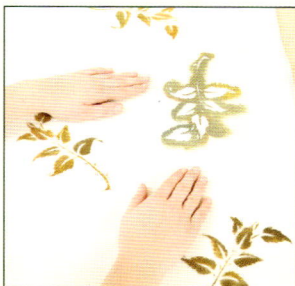

8. Reposition the stencil elsewhere on the throw and repeat the painting process until you achieve your desired effect. Once dry fix the fabric paint (see right).

Fixing Fabric Paints

When using fabric paint you will need to set the colours in some way to make the throw washable. Methods vary from brand to brand so read the manufacturer's instructions carefully first. In most cases ironing is all that is required, although sometimes salt or a chemical mordant is used instead.

Stencil Template and Colour Guide

Watering Can

A quaint and charming project: ideal for a present or the perfect thing to brighten up the dull chore of watering the garden. This project also demonstrates how easily acrylic paints can be used on metals and introduces the technique of using multiple stencils for one final image.

Materials and Equipment
Galvanised watering can, Paint brush, Paper, Sticky / masking tape, Acetate, Marker pen, Craft knife, Cutting mat, Spray glue, Old tile or container, Water and container, Stencil brush, Outdoor matt polyurethane varnish for metal

Paint: Acrylic
Blue, Red, Yellow, Green, White and Black (Use outdoor acrylic if possible)

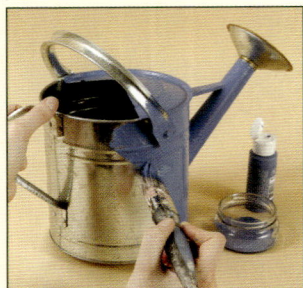

1. Paint your galvanised watering can with at least two coats of acrylic paint (ideally an outdoor acrylic paint if you can find it, but as it will be varnished it's not vital).

2. Trace or photocopy the daisy template on page 58, place under a sheet of acetate and draw over the outline of the design.

3. There are three parts to the butterfly stencil (see page 34) so that the design overlaps to produce one, intricate design. Copy each part separately onto acetate.

4. Cut out the daisy stencil and the three butterfly stencils. Make sure the butterfly stencil is cut into three sections and trim the daisy stencil to fit the can easily.

5. Spray the daisy stencil with glue and attach to the side of the watering can, smoothing down the stencil as much as possible.

6. Paint the daisy design using acrylic paints. Use an old tile as your palette and wash out your brush in between colours, particularly when painting the petals.

7. Use spray glue to stick the first butterfly stencil (with antennae) onto the can to the left of the daisy. Paint the black detail and leave to dry before removing the stencil carefully.

8. Attach the second butterfly stencil (the wings). Be careful with the position to ensure that the stencil is correctly aligned. Use a reddy-brown to paint the wings, leave to dry.

9. Glue the final stencil (with circular detail) over the previous two layers. Paint with yellow, leave to dry and remove carefully. Paint a little blue free hand on the bottom circles.

10. Reposition the daisy and butterfly stencils to repeat the design elsewhere. Paint just a single daisy on the top of the can if you don't have enough room for both.

11. The final touch is the band of cream paint around the can. Use masking tape to create straight edges. Stipple cream acrylic paint all the way round.

12. Touch up any missing or flaked sections of blue paint, allow to dry. Varnish with at least two coats of matt varnish; a wood one will do if you can't find a metal one.

Stencil Templates (continued on page 58)

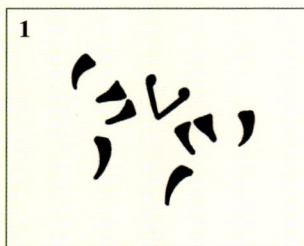

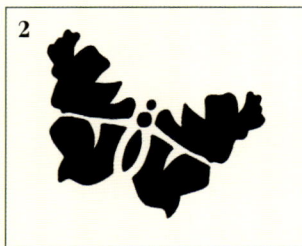

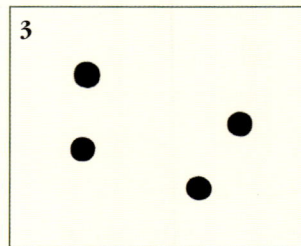

Colour Guide

Lamp Shade and Cushion

In the home, stencilling can be used to tie a decorative theme together. While stencilling on walls is one way to do this (see page 54), stencilling on key soft furnishings, like this lamp shade and cushion, can be an easier but just as effective way to achieve a similar thematic look. The lamp shade design uses acrylic paints, while the cushion uses fabric paints so the cover can be washed.

Materials and Equipment

Paper, Sticky/masking tape, Acetate, Marker pen,
Craft knife, Cutting mat, Spray glue, Plain lamp shade, Old tile,
Water and container, Plain cushion cover, Stencil brush,
Mordant (read manufacturer's instructions for how to fix the fabric paints)

Paint: Acrylic and Fabric

Blue, Red, Yellow, Green and White

1. Trace the four templates on pages 39, 40 and 59, place each copy under acetate and draw their outlines. Any alterations in size should be applied to all four layers.

2. Cut out the four sections of the blossom design. (Registration marks, see next step, could be added before cutting but they can be confusing.)

3. So the four layers will line up easily, use a copy of the complete design on page 59 and mark key points on each layer that can be matched up for positioning.

More about Registration Marks

As you mark up each stencil with registration marks make sure that you pick out points that have been painted earlier.

For instance, in this project, the branch is painted first so the second stencil with the petals should have registration marks that line up with the bends and ends of the branch. The third stencil of the leaves should mark the tips of the petals and key points along the branch, and so on.

4. Before you start to paint, plan out how many repetitions of the design you want. When happy, use spray glue to attach the branch stencil to the lamp shade.

5. Mix a dull brown, using the tile as a palette. Paint the branch using a stencil brush. Reposition the stencil and continue to paint all of the branches or just finish one design at a time.

6. When the branch is dry, remove and glue the petal stencil on top using your registration marks to line up the design. Paint the flowers with a pale pink.

7. When the petals are completely dry you can stencil the leaves. Once again, line up the stencil carefully using the registration marks then paint with a mid-green.

8. When the leaves have dried, place the final stencil on the lamp shade to paint the fine detail of the design. This last stencil is the most important one to line up correctly.

9. If you haven't repeated each stage all the way round the lamp shade then repeat the design now using the same process.

10. To make the matching cushion, make sure the cover is clean and dry. Place a plastic bag or piece of card inside the cover to prevent the paint from seeping through.

11. Reusing the stencils from the lamp shade, spray the branch stencil and stick it onto the cover. Mix up a brown that will show up well on your cushion and paint.

12. Spray and glue the flower stencil once the branch has dried. Remember to use your registration marks as before and paint with a pale pink.

13. Mix a light green and stencil the leaves, ensuring the stencil is correctly aligned before committing paint to the cover.

14. Attach the final stencil and paint the stamens with dark pink. Once dry remove the stencil and fix the fabric paint accordingly.

Stencil Templates (continued on pages 40 and 59)

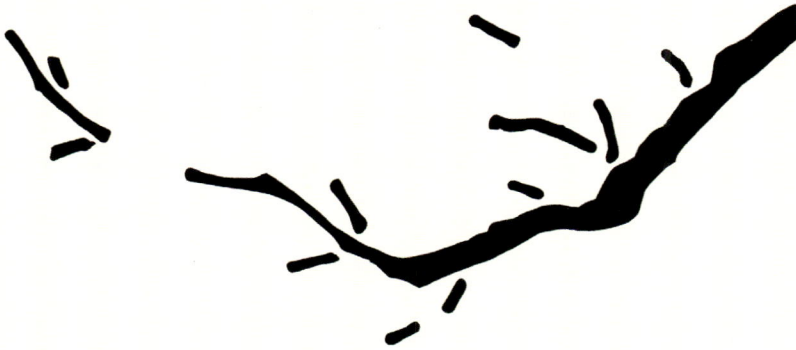

1

2

3

Colour Guide

Organza Cushion

This book has already explored stencilling on fabric using fabric paints but there are other effects that can be achieved with fabric and stencils. In this example, an enamel spray paint is used to create a delicate pattern on organza which can be added to a cushion or used as a drape.

Materials and Equipment

Plain cushion cover, Tape measure, Paper, Sticky/masking tape,
Acetate, Marker pen, Craft knife, Cutting mat,
Newspaper and kitchen paper, Organza material, Spray glue,
This project requires sewing and general sewing materials,
Blue ribbon, Burgundy ribbon, Four burgundy buttons

Paint: Spray Paint
Red metallic fast-dry enamel spray paint

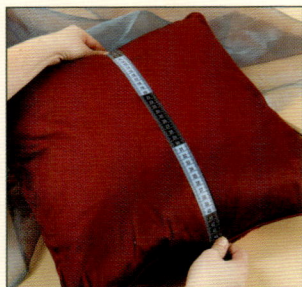

1. Measure the cushion and cut your organza to a more manageable size. Ensure you leave enough material to sew onto the cushion.

2. Trace or photocopy the template on page 44. Place this copy under a sheet of acetate and secure with sticky tape. Then draw over the design.

3. Carefully cut out the rose leaves using a craft knife. As the design is very intricate try using a scalpel or smaller craft knife.

4. Cover your entire work surface with newspaper. Place a couple of sheets of kitchen paper beneath the organza (where you will spray the paint). Spread the organza out, so there are no folds. Use the spray mount to glue the stencil on top of the fabric and the kitchen paper, smooth down firmly. Tape newspaper to the edges of the acetate to mask off the surrounding area. Spray paint will get to any unmasked area so you may prefer to practice this technique on scrap fabric first.

5. Following the manufacturer's instructions, spray the red metallic enamel paint evenly over the stencil. Leave this first coat to dry; it shouldn't take long but check the paint on the stencil rather than checking the fabric. Spray a second coat of paint evenly over the stencil. Try to spray from above, or you could even pin the newspaper and fabric up to spray from the front. Spraying from an angle may allow some of the paint to seep under the stencil. Leave to dry completely.

6. Lift the stencil and move it to extend the design in a line. Remask with newspaper and spray with two coats of metallic spray as before. Leave to dry.

Hot Tip

This project is based around a panel for a cushion but you could equally create an organza drape by continuing this pattern down the sides of a much larger piece of fabric, as pictured overleaf.

7. Pin the organza to the cover, positioning the stencil design across the middle. Fold over any excess material to create a band of material, pin either side then pin the blue ribbon in the centre of the band.

8. Fold and pin a second band on the other side of the design. On the short end fold under the organza then continue to pin the ribbon along the edge to trim it. Take the ribbon around all the edges before sewing.

9. Finish by sewing a thin burgundy ribbon on top of the blue and stitching buttons on the corners of the panel. Tie any excess ribbon in a bow to decorate.

Stencil Template

Blanket Box

Stencilling can turn the practical into a thing of beauty. This project transforms an untreated wooden chest into a stunning box that would work equally well in a bedroom, bathroom or in a nursery for storing clothes or toys.

Materials and Equipment

Untreated wooden box, White lime wash wax, Paintbrush, Paper, Sticky tape, Acetate, Marker pen, Craft knife, Cutting mat, Punch and hammer, Spray glue, Old tile, Water and container, Stencil brush, Tape measure or ruler, Wood matt varnish

Paint: Acrylic
Blue, Red, Yellow, Green, Brown and White

1. Use a lime wash wax to paint the chest a pale white (see page 15). If you're using an old chest, strip back any varnish or paint and sand down. One coat should be enough.

2. Trace or copy, enlarging as necessary, the three-part stencils for the dog rose design (pages 48 and 60) and the initials of your choice (see page 61).

3. Cut out the main sections of all four stencils, leaving the small details to be cut out with a punch (see next step). Draw on registration marks if needed, see page 37.

4. Using a punch and a small hammer, remove the circles for the pollen detail in the leaf stencil (3). If you don't have a punch, painting this detail freehand may be easier.

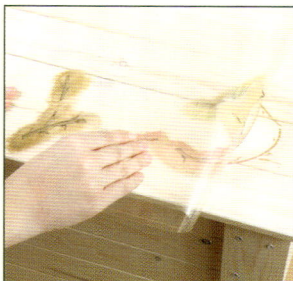

5. Spray and glue the branch stencil on one side of the chest's lid. Using the tile, mix dark brown, olive green and pale pink along the branch. Let it dry before peeling off.

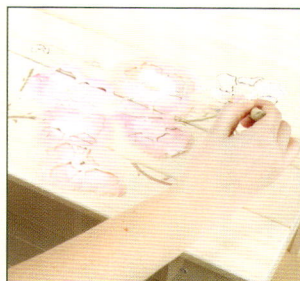

6. Glue the petal stencil over the branch making sure it is correctly aligned. Paint the roses, varying the shades of pink for a more realistic look.

7. The third stencil uses two colours, green for the leaves and yellow for the pollen. Wash your brush out between paints if you want the colours to remain true.

8. Wash all the paint off your stencils or ensure they are totally dry before flipping them over to stencil the mirror image of the design on the other side. Paint as before.

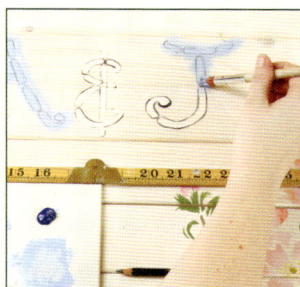

9. Spray your letter stencils with glue and stick in the middle of the two rose designs – measuring first to ensure the initials are central. Using pale blue, paint the letters.

10. Add more white to your blue paint then use this paler colour to stencil the ampersand. Allow the acrylic to dry then carefully peel off the acetate.

11. Once all of your designs are completely dry paint the entire box with at least two coats of matt varnish and leave to dry once again before use.

Stencil Templates (continued on page 60) and Colour Guide

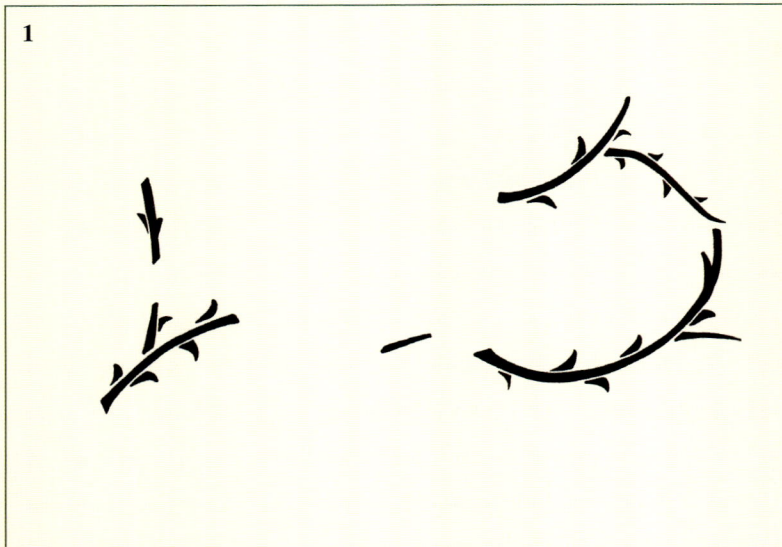

1

Nursery Chair

A charming gift or a great way to personalise you own child's nursery, this chair is really pretty and will help develop your practical skills. The design could easily be adapted to make delightful kitchen chairs if you think they're too nice for the kids!

Materials and Equipment

Untreated wooden chair, Sand paper, Magnolia emulsion, Paintbrush, Paper, Sticky/masking tape, Acetate, Marker pen, Craft knife, Cutting mat, Punch and hammer, Spray glue, Old tile, Water and container, Stencil brush, Wood matt varnish

Paint: Acrylic
Blue, Red, Yellow, Green and White

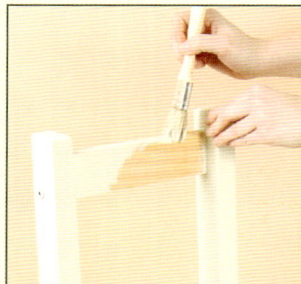

1. Depending on the surface of your wood, clean and sand the chair first. Then, paint the chair with at least two coats of magnolia emulsion paint, leave to dry.

2. Copy the templates on pages 52, 61 and 62 and enlarge to fit the seat of the chair. Trace the copies of each stencil using the name of your choice.

3. Cut out the ribbon and stalk details, the bow and the name stencils. Mark the stencils with registration points if necessary. See step 4 for cutting the petals.

4. Use a punch and hammer to create the holes for the pollen. Then use an even smaller punch to cut circles for the petal tips, and a knife to cut the rest of the petal.

5. Trim the corners of the stencils so they fit neatly into the seat. Attach the main daisy stencil first with the spray glue and paint the white flowers and green stems.

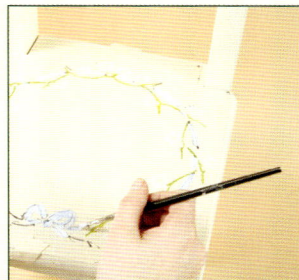

6. Once the paint from the previous stencil has dried, peel off and replace with the ribbon stencil. Mix a light blue and paint the ribbon detail.

7. As before, wait for the paint to dry then attach the last of the daisy chain stencils. Paint the pollen of the flowers with yellow. If you wish you can add a little pink as well.

8. To paint the rainbow effect of the name mix a green and stencil this all the way along the bottom of the letters. Overlap the green with pink and so on as pictured.

9. With the seat finished you can now paint the small bow detail on either side of the back support and paint each panel beneath the seat with a pale blue.

Colour Guide

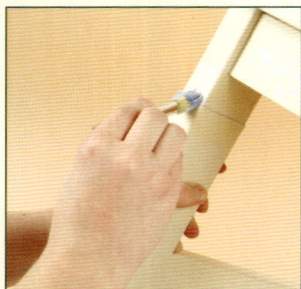

10. Tape strips of masking tape around the legs of the chair to create one band around the top of each leg and one at the bottom. Paint these with the pale blue.

11. Once all the paint has dried, varnish the chair with at least two coats, or more, depending on the type of varnish.

Stencil Templates (continued on pages 61 and 62)

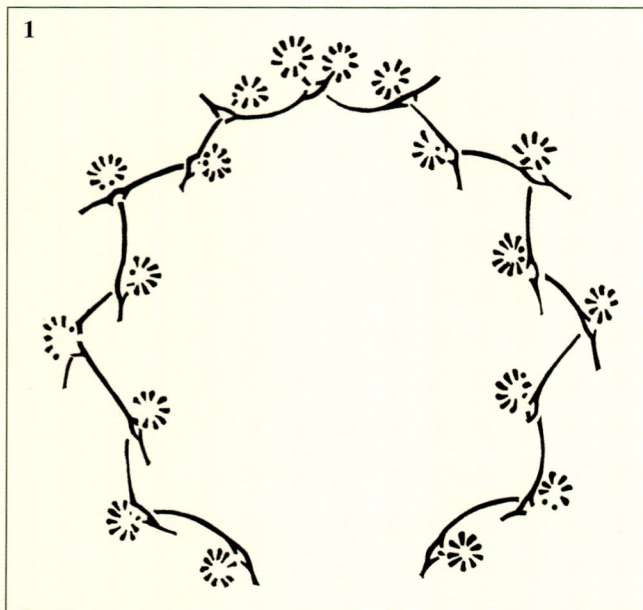

1

52

Ivy Trellis

An ivy design is a classic motif for stencilling as it can suit almost any room. Here the stencilling has been used within panels which help contain the design and prevent it from being too overpowering.

Materials and Equipment

Matt emulsion, Paintbrush, Masking/sticky tape, Spirit level,
Tape measure or ruler, Pencil, Paper, Acetate, Marker pen, Craft knife,
Cutting mat, Paint containers, Water and container, Stencil brush,
Spray glue, Decorators acrylic matt varnish, Thick paint brush

Paint: Acrylic

Blue, Yellow Ochre, Green, Brown and White

1. Prepare your wall surface (see pages 18–19). Paint the wall with your chosen matt emulsion. When dry mask off rectangular panels and paint a 2 cm border.

2. Measure each panel into even squares using a spirit measure and plumb line to ensure the lines are straight. You will use these squares to create a diamond trellis pattern with the ivy.

3. Measure the diagonal of your square and copy and enlarge the ivy template to this size. Trace the outline with a marker pen as normal.

4. Using a craft knife carefully cut out your ivy stencil on a cutting mat. As you may be using this one stencil extensively you may want to make spares in case of tears.

5. Mix your paint for the stencil in your containers, make sure you mix enough to paint the whole wall, or at least a panel at a time so the colour remains consistent.

6. Using spray glue, mount the stencil on the wall working along the diagonal of each square as pictured.

7. Begin painting the ivy; use a lighter, more yellow, colour to paint the stalks of the ivy and part of the leaves.

8. Paint the rest of the leaves with the darker green colour. Allow this colour to blend with the first.

9. Should your design fall slightly short of the corner, remove the stencil and reposition it, matching up the design, to extend the pattern.

10. Reposition the stencil in the square below, working along the diagonal again, and paint as before.

11. Begin to paint the crossing diagonals. Paint just as before but omit colouring some of the leaves so that the designs don't overlap. Repeat the pattern to complete each panel.

12. Once the whole design is complete and dry, paint over the stencil work with a decorator's matt varnish to protect it. Repeat with further coats as needed.

Stencil Template and Colour Guide

Additional Templates

If you've completed some of the projects prior to this section you'll be eager to try out even more designs. Here you'll find some of the designs already featured and additional ones that can be used in any number of ways.

Watering Can Stencil Template (pages 32–35)

Additional Designs

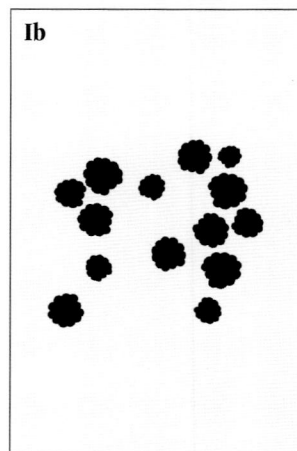

Ia

Ib

Lamp Shade Template (pages 36–41)

4

Lamp Shade Registration Template

Blanket Box Stencil Templates (pages 46–49)

Additional Designs

2

IIa

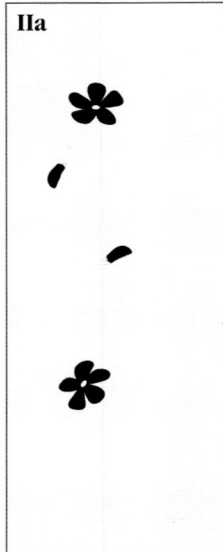

3

IIb

Alphabet Stencil Templates

a b c d e f g h i
j k l m n o p q r
s t u v w x y z

A B C D E F G H I
J K L M N O P Q R
S T U V W X Y Z

1 2 3 4 5 6 7 8 9
0 . , ¢ ! ?

Nursery Chair Templates (pages 50–53)

Additional Designs

2

3

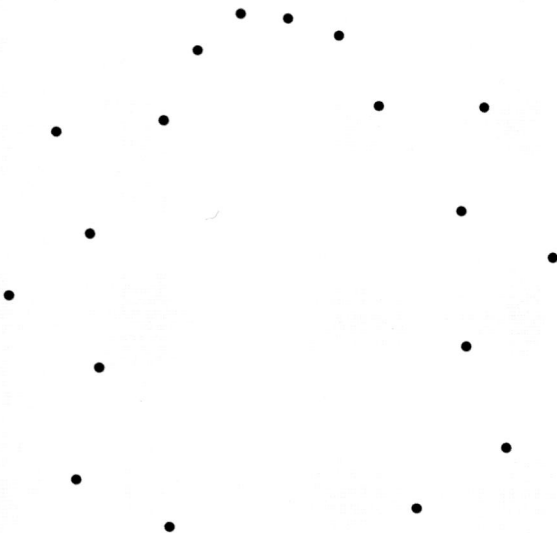

IIIa

IIIb

IIIc

Nursery Chair Registration Template (pages 50–53)

Blanket Box Registration Template (pages 46–49)

Conclusion

Completing the array of projects in this book should have shown you the versatility of stencilling. Even by using just acrylic or fabric paints, you can create imaginative and memorable designs – but there are still a wealth of projects out there just waiting to be made.

As your skills improve, you should try to broaden your supply of materials, and try out specialist paints to get even better and more varied results.

Refer back to the preparation and finishing section and try out some of the advanced finishes that are listed such as crackle varnishes – you'll be surprised at how different your stencils can look. Alternatively, why not experiment with varnish. For example, layers of gloss varnish, rubbed down in between coats will build up to create a beautiful

lacquered effect similar to that produced by cabinet makers. The best effects, however, will be those you discover yourself so have fun finding them.

Designing your own stencils can be great fun too. Take note of your surroundings, look for inspiration from nature, magazines or television, or try following some of our future project ideas. Whatever task you take on next it's sure to be just the beginning of a creative interest that will keep you occupied for years to come.

THE COUNTRY DIARY®

Other titles available in the range are:

The Country Diary of an Edwardian Lady

Painting with Watercolours

Stencilling

Herbal Remedies

Calligraphy

Flower Pressing

Cross Stitch

Learn to Paint Wildlife

Learn to Draw Nature

www.kudosbooks.com